Facts About the Jaguar

By Lisa Strattin

© 2019 Lisa Strattin

FREE BOOK

FREE FOR ALL SUBSCRIBERS

LisaStrattin.com/Subscribe-Here

BOX SET

- **FACTS ABOUT THE POISON DART FROGS**
- **FACTS ABOUT THE THREE TOED SLOTH**
- **FACTS ABOUT THE RED PANDA**
- **FACTS ABOUT THE SEAHORSE**
- **FACTS ABOUT THE PLATYPUS**
- **FACTS ABOUT THE REINDEER**
- **FACTS ABOUT THE PANTHER**
- **FACTS ABOUT THE SIBERIAN HUSKY**

LisaStrattin.com/BookBundle

Facts for Kids Picture Books by Lisa Strattin

Little Blue Penguin, Vol 92

Chipmunk, Vol 5

Frilled Lizard, Vol 39

Blue and Gold Macaw, Vol 13

Poison Dart Frogs, Vol 50

Blue Tarantula, Vol 115

African Elephants, Vol 8

Amur Leopard, Vol 89

Sabre Tooth Tiger, Vol 167

Baboon, Vol 174

Sign Up for New Release Emails Here

LisaStrattin.com/subscribe-here

Contents

INTRODUCTION

The Jaguar is the largest feline on the American continent. They are closely related to Leopards and have a number of similar characteristics, including the distinctive spotted pattern on their fur. They are the third biggest cat in the world behind the Tiger and the Lion and are well known for their immense power and agility.

The name Jaguar is said to come from the Native American word yaguar which means "he who kills with one leap".

CHARACTERISTICS

Although this animal spends most of its time resting in the safety of the trees or hunting in the dense undergrowth, they love to be in the close proximity of water. They rarely roam into arid, more desert-like areas. The Jaguar is an excellent swimmer and can move through the water at great speed, especially when in pursuit of prey. They are a solitary animal except for the first couple of years of life that is spent spend with their mother.

Jaguars have the strongest bite force of all Cats and like other "big Cats" they can roar.

APPEARANCE

The Jaguar is a large, muscular animal with a heavier and sturdier body than that of a Leopard. They have a large, broad head with strong jaws. They tend to have a cover of either tan or dark yellow fur, which is dotted with darker rose-like patterns that are similar to those of a Leopard. Known as *rosetting*, the pattern on their fur is unique to each animal, like fingerprints are unique to individual people, and despite the beauty, these spots actually act as the perfect camouflage in the surrounding jungle.

Although Jaguars usually have yellowish-colored fur, they have also been seen as black and white. As with black Leopards, they are not completely black because you can still see the faint spotting in strong sunlight.

REPRODUCTION

Despite the fact that most Jaguar cubs are generally born between the months of December and March, they are sometimes born at other times of the year. During the mating season, the female uses loud vocal calls to attract a male into her territory.

Females typically give birth to two or three cubs at a time. Once the cubs are born, the female will not allow any male in her territory, becoming very protective of her young. Jaguar cubs are born blind and will be able to see after about two weeks. They are weaned by their mother when they are 3 months old or so. However, the cubs rely on their mother to hunt and provide food until they are about 6 months of age. At 6 months old, the cubs start to go with the mother on hunts but will not go out on their own until they are one to two years old and have established their own home territory.

LIFE SPAN

Jaguars live for an average of 12 to 15 years.

SIZE

An adult Jaguar can grow to be as long as 6 feet and can weigh up to 350 pounds!

It is really a very BIG CAT!

HABITAT

Males are particularly territorial and although their home range will overlap those of a number of females, they will defend their patch fiercely from other males. Jaguars mark their territories with urine, by scratching marks onto trees, and asserting themselves with growling vocal calls.

They primarily live in the tropical rainforests of Central and South America. Historically, the range of the Jaguar stretched across the whole continent and even into the southern states of the USA, but they are today confined to remote pockets of rainforest areas of the moist Amazon Basin.

They tend to prefer thick, dense, moist jungle regions where there is plenty of cover so that they can to successfully hunt and then ambush prey. They are generally found close to water and like permanent swampland and seasonally flooded forests.

DIET

The majority of a Jaguar's hunting is done on the ground but they are also known to hunt in the water and from the trees. They like to ambush prey, often killing it with one powerful bite.

Medium-sized mammals make up the majority of their diet. This includes: deer, Capybara, Peccaries and Tapirs, which they stalk quietly through the jungle. When in the water, they hunt turtles, fish and even small Caiman (a reptile, like an alligator or crocodile) when they find them.

ENEMIES

Due to the large size and dominant nature of the Jaguar, there are no other wild animals that are known to actually consider it as prey.

SUITABILITY AS PETS

Certainly, the Jaguar is not suitable to be a house pet. If you would like to see them, you can check out your local zoo (if you have one) to see if they have a habitat where you can get a good look at these beautiful Big Cats.

COLOR ME

COLOR ME

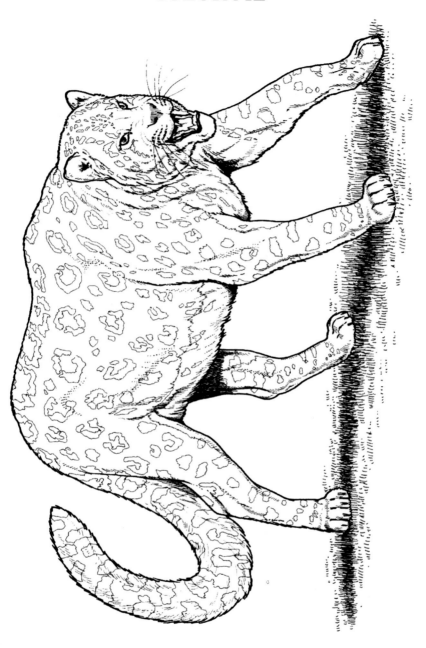

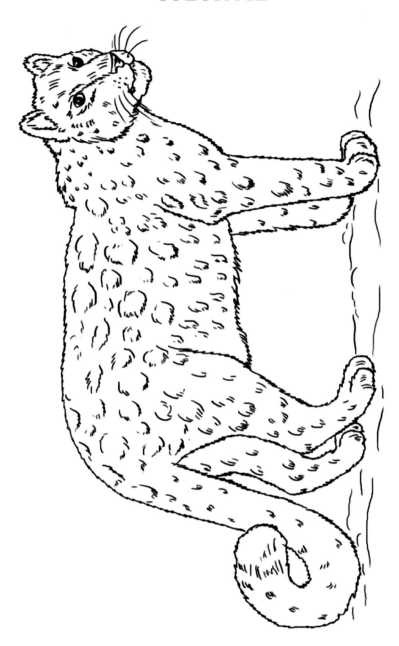

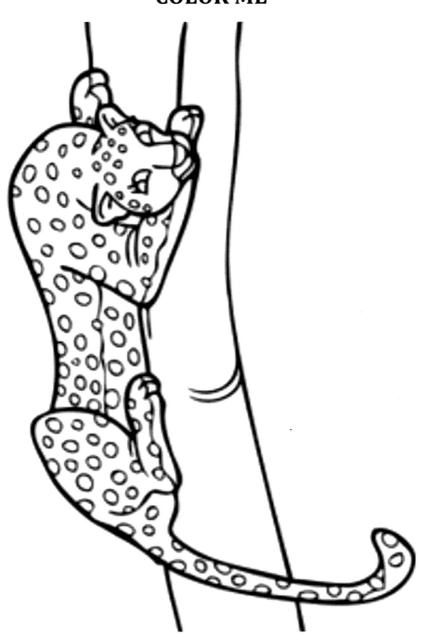

COLOR ME

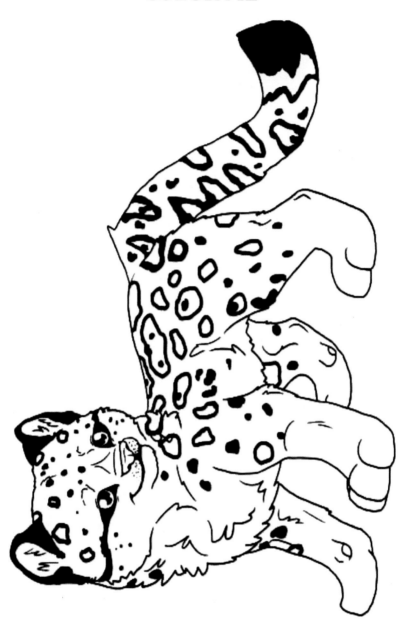

Please leave me a review here:

LisaStrattin.com/Review-Vol-286

For more Kindle Downloads Visit Lisa Strattin
Author Page on Amazon Author Central

amazon.com/author/lisastrattin

To see upcoming titles, visit my website at
LisaStrattin.com– most books available on Kindle!

LisaStrattin.com

FREE BOOK

FOR ALL SUBSCRIBERS – SIGN UP NOW

LisaStrattin.com/Subscribe-Here

LisaStrattin.com/Facebook

LisaStrattin.com/Youtube